OLD TESTAMENT WITNESS

Written & Designed by
Doug Powell

תורה נביאים וכתובים

BIBLIA HEBRAICA
ACCURATISSIMA,
Notis Hebraïcis
et Lemmatibus Latinis illustrata.

A

JOHANNE LEUSDEN,
Philosophiæ Doctore, &
Linguæ Sanctæ in Academia
Ultrajectina Professore.

AMSTELODAMI,
Typis et sumptibus
JOSEPHI ATHIAS.
Anno, CIƆ IƆC LXVII.

Published by
Apologia Educational Ministries, Inc.
1106 Meridian Plaza, Suite 220/340
Anderson, IN. 46016
Manufactured in the USA
First Printing: May, 2014

✝apologia

OLD TESTAMENT WITNESS

Written & Designed by
Doug Powell

The teachings of Jesus are the basis of all Christian thought. They are the guides and rules for how we should live and how we should worship. The books that contain his teaching are called the New Testament. But Christians have far more books in their Bibles than the New Testament books. In fact, most of the Bible is made up of the Hebrew scriptures, what Christians call the Old Testament. The reason for this is that even though Christ is the ultimate authority for Christians, he taught that the Hebrew scriptures are God's revealed word and are an authority for our lives. Not only that, but he is the fulfillment of the promises the Old Testament makes about the coming messiah, he is what the system of temple sacrifices and ceremonial laws pointed to, and he himself is the fulfillment of the law. In other words, in order to fully understand who Jesus is requires that we explore the Hebrew scriptures.

AboutBibleVideos.com

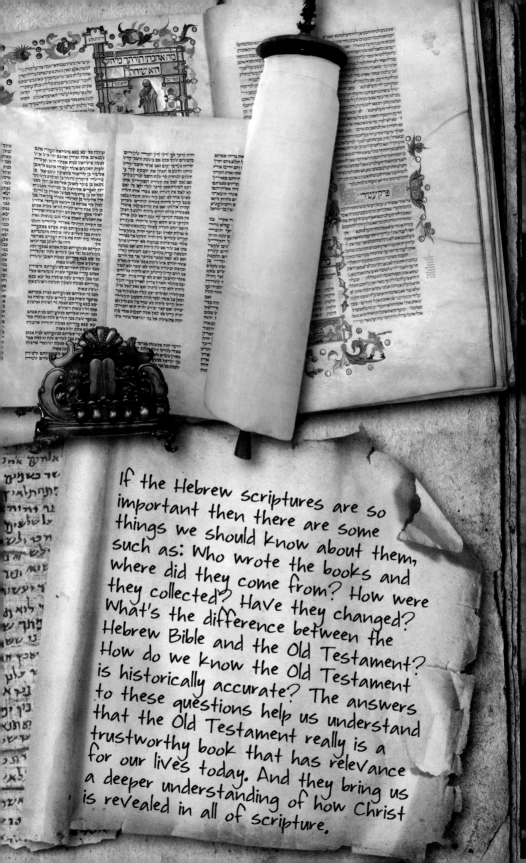

If the Hebrew scriptures are so important then there are some things we should know about them, such as: Who wrote the books and where did they come from? How were they collected? Have they changed? What's the difference between the Hebrew Bible and the Old Testament? How do we know the Old Testament is historically accurate? The answers to these questions help us understand that the Old Testament really is a trustworthy book that has relevance for our lives today. And they bring us a deeper understanding of how Christ is revealed in all of scripture.

Unlike the New Testament, which is well-known for having more original-language manuscripts than any other ancient book, there are not very many ancient manuscripts of the Old Testament. This might seem strange since the Hebrew Bible is so much older than the New Testament, and therefore there could be many more copies. But the Jews had a different way of thinking about copies of scripture than modern historians. We think of the oldest copies being the best and most reliable because they are closer to the original writings than other copies. But Jewish scribes prefer the newest copies because they are the least likely to be damaged or flawed or have some blemish on the text. This is why most of the oldest copies of the Hebrew Bible are no earlier than the Middle Ages.

Copy of the Babylonian Talmud

Any time a copy of the Hebrew Bible is damaged or replaced it is buried during a special ceremony – that's how highly the Jews think of scripture. The reason why there are not a lot of ancient copies of the Old Testament is because the Jews got rid of them in order to protect the text by using only the best copies they had. After a copy has been replaced it is put in a special place called a "genizah," where it will stay (often for many years) until a burial ceremony is held. Many of our oldest copies were found in the genizahs of synagogues.

Fragments of a Torah scroll found in the genizah of the Cairo Synagogue around 1896.

In addition to original language manuscripts, there are other sources that recover the original text of the Old Testament. One of the most important is the Septuagint, a Greek translation made 250–150 BC. Another valuable source is the Latin Vulgate, a translation made by Jerome and completed in the early fifth century. Paraphrases and commentaries, called Targums, by early Jewish theologians are yet another way that is useful for recovering the original text. The Samaritan Pentateuch is also helpful, even though the Samaritans were a heretical sect of Judaism and edited the text to fit their unorthodox beliefs.

COPYING

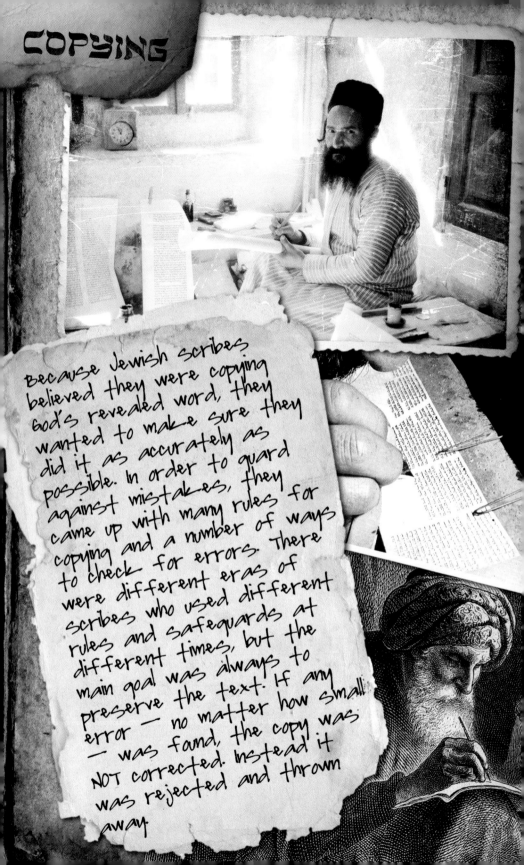

Because Jewish scribes believed they were copying God's revealed word, they wanted to make sure they did it as accurately as possible. In order to guard against mistakes, they came up with many rules for copying and a number of ways to check for errors. There were different eras of scribes who used different rules and safeguards at different times, but the main goal was always to preserve the text. If any error — no matter how small — was found, the copy was NOT corrected. Instead it was rejected and thrown away

The Talmudist tradition of scribes copied the text during the time starting around the fall of Jerusalem in AD 70 to about 500. Their techniques included creating a kind of grid on the page of a codex. The grid made it easier to make sure there were always thirty characters on each line, and between 48 to 60 lines in each column. They also made sure each page had the same number of columns of text. There were even rules for how much space had to be left between the lines of text, the characters, and the section breaks. No letter could ever touch another letter. The Torah (the first five books of the Hebrew Bible) had to end at the end of a line with no spaces in the grid for that line left empty. Nothing could be written from memory, not even a word; the scribes copied one letter at a time. There was even a special recipe for the ink. And the scribe had to follow rules about bathing as well as wearing certain clothes.

Materials used to make ink for copying scripture

The Masoretic scribes were active between AD 500 and 900. Some of their safeguards including counting the number of words and letters in each book. They also counted to the middle letter and middle word in the book to make sure it matched the one they were copying. They were so meticulous they even knew how many times each letter was in each book. They left four blank lines between each book. The Masoretes also wanted to make sure the proper pronunciation wasn't lost over time, which was a problem because the Hebrew alphabet has no vowels. So the Masoretes developed a system of dots above and below the letters that are vowels used to help with pronunciation.

CANON CRITERIA

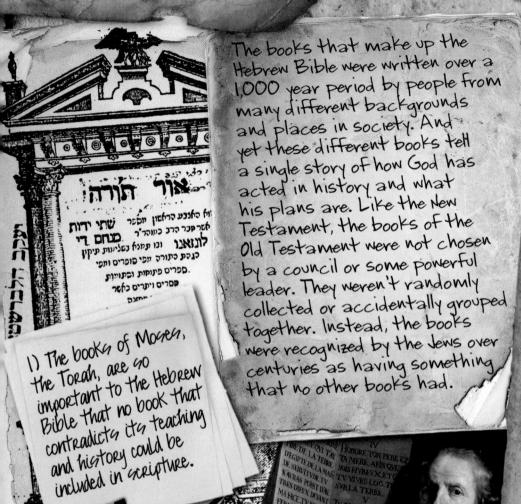

The books that make up the Hebrew Bible were written over a 1,000 year period by people from many different backgrounds and places in society. And yet these different books tell a single story of how God has acted in history and what his plans are. Like the New Testament, the books of the Old Testament were not chosen by a council or some powerful leader. They weren't randomly collected or accidentally grouped together. Instead, the books were recognized by the Jews over centuries as having something that no other books had.

1) The books of Moses, the Torah, are so important to the Hebrew Bible that no book that contradicts its teaching and history could be included in scripture.

2) From Moses to Malachi (c. 435 BC, the time of Ezra and Nehemiah) there was an unbroken chain of prophets. No writing after that time could be included in scripture since there was no prophet to write under the power of inspiration. According to Jewish tradition, every book in the Hebrew Bible was written by a prophet.

3) The writing had to be in Hebrew (though there are a few passages of Aramaic)

4) The writing had to be known throughout Jewish communities.

The very first part of the Hebrew Bible to be written was the Ten Commandments, which were etched in stone by the very finger of God. Although, the prophets declared the word of God, they also wrote down the things God had given them to say. All throughout scripture are verses that attribute certain writings to certain prophets. And every time a prophet wrote, their writing was added to the canon. When the line of prophets ended with Malachi, the canon was complete.

TANAKH

The twenty-two books of the Tanakh contain the exact same text as the Old Testament, but the books are divided differently. Jews do not refer to their Bible as "The Old Testament," of course. For them, there is only one testament, often called the Hebrew Bible. Another name for it is the "Tanakh." This name is an anagram that comes from each of the three sections of the Bible.

Torah
The first five books are called the Torah. They were written by Moses and are the books that other books in the canon must conform to.

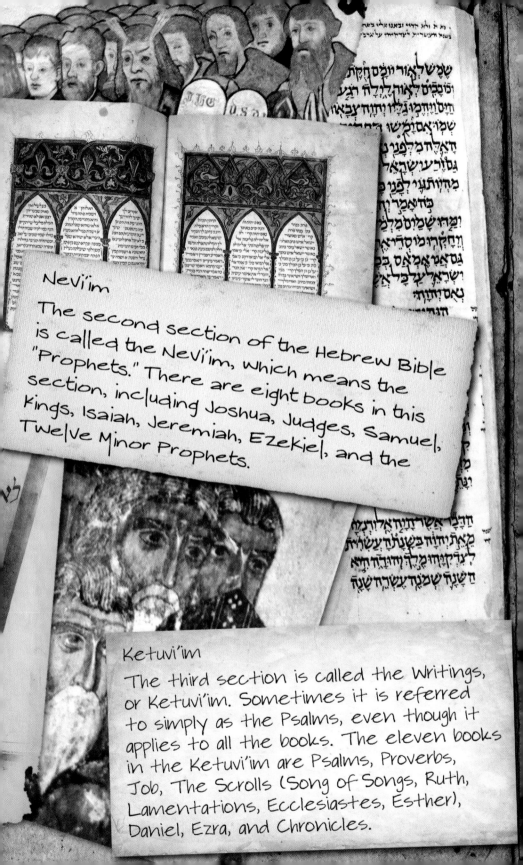

Nevi'im

The second section of the Hebrew Bible is called the Nevi'im, which means the "Prophets." There are eight books in this section, including Joshua, Judges, Samuel, Kings, Isaiah, Jeremiah, Ezekiel, and the Twelve Minor Prophets.

Ketuvi'im

The third section is called the Writings, or Ketuvi'im. Sometimes it is referred to simply as the Psalms, even though it applies to all the books. The eleven books in the Ketuvi'im are Psalms, Proverbs, Job, The Scrolls (Song of Songs, Ruth, Lamentations, Ecclesiastes, Esther), Daniel, Ezra, and Chronicles.

CANON FORMATION

When Jerusalem was destroyed by the Romans in AD 70, the Jews were left without a temple and began to move to other parts of the world. In order to preserve as much of Judaism as possible, the leaders wanted to make sure that as people of the book they all had the same book. At this point, most Christians were Jewish, and therefore used the same scriptures, usually the Greek translation called the Septuagint. To separate themselves from Christians, the Jews decided to stop using the Septuagint and go back to a standardized Hebrew text.

There are several ancient sources that show that even 100 years before the birth of Jesus, the canon was closed and the books agreed upon.

1 Maccabees, a book containing Jewish history from about 160 BC, says there were no prophets at that time: "So there was great distress in Israel, su as had not been since the time that prophets ceased to appear among them." (1 Maccabees 9:27, RSV) Passages in 4:45-46 and 14:41 also indicate there were no prophets in Israel.

FLAVII JOSEPHI
Noodgevende
Joodsche Historien
e Boecken
Niet
EGESIPPUS
vande endige Verstoring
der Stadt
JERUSALEM.

10th century copy of 1 Maccabees

Josephus, a Jewish Roman historian from the first century AD, wrote "For we have not an innumerable multitude of books among us, disagreeing from and contradicting one another, [as the Greeks have] but only twenty-two books, which contain the records of all the past times; which are justly believed to be divine; and of them five belong to Moses, which contain his laws and the traditions of the origin of mankind till his death.

This interval of time was little short of three thousand years; but as to the time from the death of Moses till the reign of Artaxerxes King of Persia, who reigned after Xerxes, the prophets, who were after Moses, wrote down what was done in their times in thirteen books. The remaining four books contain hymns to God, and precepts for the conduct of human life." (Against Apian 1.8)

The Babylonian Talmud, which contains the most important traditions taught by rabbis around the time of Christ, says "Our Rabbis taught Since the death of the last prophets, Haggai, Zechariah and Malachi, the Holy Spirit [of prophetic inspiration] departed from Israel; yet they were still able to avail themselves of the Bath-Kol." (Tractate Sanhedrin Folio 11a, 30 BC – AD 10)

Other writings such as 2 Baruch 85:1-2 and Azariah 3 also state there were no prophets at this time. And the Babylonian Talmud Baba Bathra Tractate 1 not only lists the books but gives their order.

SEPTUAGINT

After Alexander the Great successfully brought Greek culture to the lands he conquered, many Jews became less familiar with Hebrew. Around 250 BC, the Jewish population in Alexandria, Egypt, grew large enough that Ptolemy Philadelphus asked Eleazar, the high priest at the time, to send 72 scholars to translate the Hebrew Bible into Greek. The name Septuagint means "seventy," and comes from the number of translators. Sometimes it is referred to as the LXX. This is the version of the Bible that Jesus and his disciples used and quoted from. By the end of the first century AD the Jews were not happy that the Septuagint had become adopted by Christians, and that helped lead the way to a new, standardized Hebrew text.

When the text was translated, many of the books were divided. Samuel, Kings, Chronicles, and Ezra (which included Nehemiah) were divided into two books each. The five books in the Scrolls each became their own book. The twelve books of the Minor Prophets each became their own, as well. That made the number of books 39 instead of 22. Also, instead of the three sections, it was broken into four: law, history, poetry, and prophecy. The Old Testament uses the book divisions, titles, and order of the Septuagint, but uses the Masoretic text as the basis of translation.

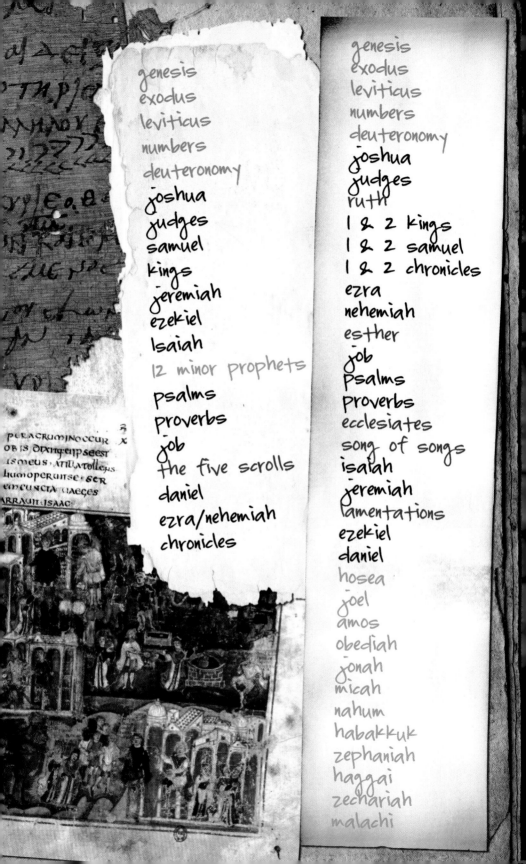

genesis
exodus
leviticus
numbers
deuteronomy
joshua
judges
samuel
kings
jeremiah
ezekiel
Isaiah
12 minor prophets
psalms
proverbs
job
the five scrolls
daniel
ezra/nehemiah
chronicles

genesis
exodus
leviticus
numbers
deuteronomy
joshua
judges
ruth
1 & 2 kings
1 & 2 samuel
1 & 2 chronicles
ezra
nehemiah
esther
job
psalms
proverbs
ecclesiates
song of songs
isaiah
jeremiah
lamentations
ezekiel
daniel
hosea
joel
amos
obediah
jonah
micah
nahum
habakkuk
zephaniah
haggai
zechariah
malachi

PLRACRUMINOCCUR x
OB IS Ɔpinguplseest
ismeus. Atillatolleus
humoperuitse SCR
eincuncta uaeges
ARRAuit ISAAC

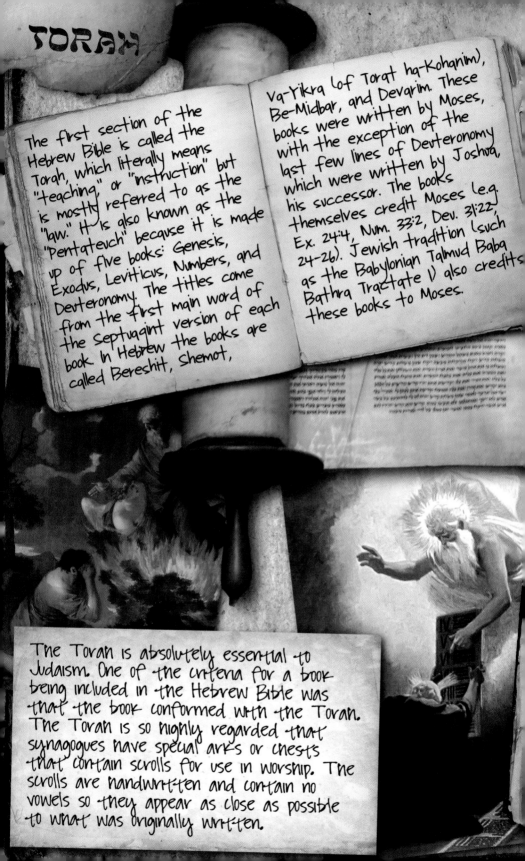

TORAH

The first section of the Hebrew Bible is called the Torah, which literally means "teaching," or "instruction" but is mostly referred to as the "law." It is also known as the "Pentateuch" because it is made up of five books: Genesis, Exodus, Leviticus, Numbers, and Deuteronomy. The titles come from the first main word of the Septuagint version of each book. In Hebrew the books are called Bereshit, Shemot, Va-Yikra (of Torat ha-Kohanim), Be-Midbar, and Devarim. These books were written by Moses, with the exception of the last few lines of Deuteronomy which were written by Joshua, his successor. The books themselves credit Moses (e.g. Ex. 24:4, Num. 33:2, Deu. 31:22, 24-26). Jewish tradition (such as the Babylonian Talmud Baba Bathra Tractate 1) also credits these books to Moses.

The Torah is absolutely essential to Judaism. One of the criteria for a book being included in the Hebrew Bible was that the book conformed with the Torah. The Torah is so highly regarded that synagogues have special arks or chests that contain scrolls for use in worship. The scrolls are handwritten and contain no vowels so they appear as close as possible to what was originally written.

One of the reasons why the Torah is so important is because Moses could prove he was a prophet, that he had the authority to speak for God. Prophets are not people who tell the future, but people God uses to speak through. But the people needed a way to recognize that someone was a prophet, so God provided a way to authenticate prophets by giving them miraculous signs and wonders.

Although Moses is credited with writing Genesis, the events that were recorded didn't happen during his lifetime. Scholars have tried to explain this many different ways. Some claim that Moses didn't write any of it or that it is nothing more than legend. Others point out whoever wrote it borrowed older stories from other cultures and that Genesis is a Jewish version of the stories. The vast majority of the time these views are held because the scholars don't believe in inspiration or miracles. The traditional view that Moses wrote Genesis does not mean he didn't use stories from other cultures or wasn't inspired. Most of the time the Holy Spirit did not dictate words to Moses, but gave him a message and protected Moses from error as he wrote the books in his own words and decided what material to use for the parts of history that happened before his time. Some things could only come from the Spirit, such as the creation account. Others might have come from different histories or even Jewish writings that existed before Moses but have since been lost.

PROPHETS

As the first writing prophet, Moses became the example for how to recognize a prophet. If their miraculous sign was a prophecy about the future, then at least one prophecy had to come true during his lifetime. And prophets could NEVER be wrong when they foretold something. If they were ever wrong they were stoned to death. They didn't do these these signs and wonders through their own power or to make themselves famous or look good. They did them to get the attention of people so they would listen the their message. Moses was also very public and did these things openly for all to see. All other prophets followed Moses in this way.

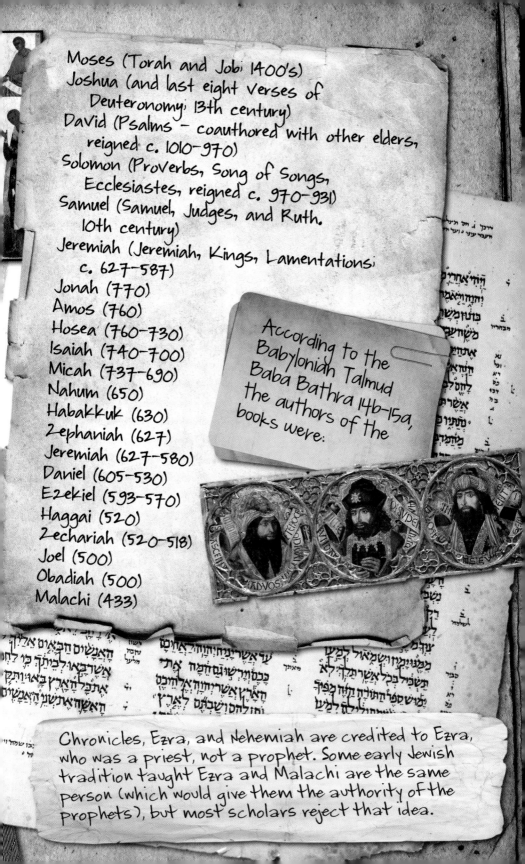

Moses (Torah and Job, 1400's)

Joshua (and last eight verses of
   Deuteronomy, 13th century)

David (Psalms — coauthored with other elders,
   reigned c. 1010–970)

Solomon (Proverbs, Song of Songs,
   Ecclesiastes, reigned c. 970–931)

Samuel (Samuel, Judges, and Ruth,
   10th century)

Jeremiah (Jeremiah, Kings, Lamentations,
   c. 627–587)

Jonah (770)

Amos (760)

Hosea (760–730)

Isaiah (740–700)

Micah (737–690)

Nahum (650)

Habakkuk (630)

Zephaniah (627)

Jeremiah (627–580)

Daniel (605–530)

Ezekiel (593–570)

Haggai (520)

Zechariah (520–518)

Joel (500)

Obadiah (500)

Malachi (433)

According to the
Babylonian Talmud
Baba Bathra 14b–15a,
the authors of the
books were:

Chronicles, Ezra, and Nehemiah are credited to Ezra,
who was a priest, not a prophet. Some early Jewish
tradition taught Ezra and Malachi are the same
person (which would give them the authority of the
prophets), but most scholars reject that idea.

DOCUMENTARY HYPOTHESIS

Not everyone believes Moses wrote the Torah. In the middle of the 1800s, German biblical scholars began to see things in the text that they thought showed the Torah was written by several people at different times. They thought that because different passages emphasized certain things that they could not have been written by the same person. And they tried to break these passages into categories based on certain words and ideas that they used. The other thing they noticed was that sometimes there are two accounts of the same event told in different ways, such as the creation stories in Genesis 1 and 2. These scholars thought the best explanation was that the Torah had been edited together from several different writings, each written from a different perspective. This theory is called the Documentary Hypothesis.

THE NAME OF THE LORD

The four sources of the Torah were called J, E, P, and D. The first two get their names from how they refer to God. "J" stands for YHWH, the personal name of God, which is transliterated from Hebrew to German using the letter J. "E" stands for Elohim, a more generic term meaning god (without a capital "G"). "D" stands for Deuteronomist since most of this writing is found in that book. "P" is for priest and has to do with the writing focused on worship.

One of the easiest ways to show some of the different sources is to look at Genesis 1, 2 and 5. Genesis 1:1 – 2:4a is credited to "J," the Yahwehist, as is Genesis 5. The material in between those sections is credited to the Elohimist. This is a good example of J using "YHWH" and E using "Elohim." J says the world was created, but E says it was formed. J uses the phrase "male and female," but E says "man and woman." And Genesis 5 goes back to using YHWH, which is why it is not credited to E.

But sometimes the division of sources gets very complicated, as in the account of the Flood. Gen 6:5–8; 7:1–5, 7–8, 10, 12, 16b–17, 22–23; 8:2b–3, 6–12, 3b, and 2–22 are credited to J. But Gen 6:9–13, 14–22; 7:6, 9, 11, 13–16a, 18–21, 24; 8:1–2a, 4–5, 13a, 14–17; 9:1–19 are credited to P. And if that isn't complicated enough, as the Documentary Hypothesis has developed, more scholars find more sources. For example, some see several different priests, each with his own category.

Jewish Priest

Interestingly, the identification of more sources has revealed a huge problem with the theory, and that is identifying the sources says more about the presuppositions of the scholar than it does about the text itself. As a result, this way of reading the text is far less popular than it once was. It's far more likely that Moses was emphasizing different things in different passages and therefore used different terms to do it. But the biggest problem with the theory is that the scholars who believe it think the Bible was written by man and was not inspired by God.

COVENANTS
AND NEAR EAST TREATIES

Throughout the Hebrew Bible we see God making a people for himself by using covenants. Noah, Abraham, Moses, and David all entered into covenants with God. There are also less obvious covenants with Adam and even in the creation event itself. And there are times these covenants are remembered or recommitted to through Isaac, Jacob and others.

Sometimes a covenant is misunderstood to be like a contract, but there are are important differences. But these differences were hard to fully understand until recently. Archaeological discoveries have revealed that covenants were common throughout the world of the ancient Near East. They were often used to make treaties to avoid war. Unlike a contract, these covenants/treaties were between two unequal parties. One was a powerful king, called a suzerain (or Lord), and the other was a lesser king, called a vassal (or servant). If a suzerain wanted to conquer the kingdom of a lesser king, instead of attacking it and destroying valuable property, the suzerain could impose a treaty on the vassal king.

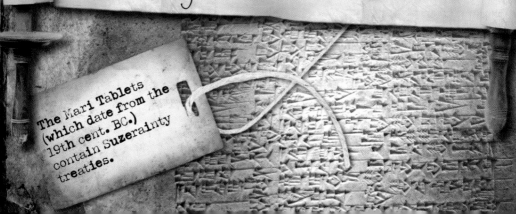

The Mari Tablets (which date from the 19th cent. BC.) contain Suzerainty treaties.

All of the rules of the covenant would be set by the suzerain, and the vassal represented all of his people including future generations. If the vassal kept the terms then the people would be blessed. If the vassal did not, the people would receive curses. The form of Suzerainty treaties changed over time, which helps scholars date them, but the general form is consistent. The parties are named, their history is given, the terms are given, the blessings and curses are given, and it is ratified and read. Then, two copies are made, usually on stone, and are placed in the sanctuaries of worship for each kingdom.

One of the Amarna Letters from the 14th cent. BC. Some of the tablets contain Suzerainty treaties.

The reason these treaties are important is because the biblical covenants seem to borrow heavily from Suzerainty treaties. In fact, Deuteronomy can be outlined in the treaty form listed above. Liberal scholars have claimed that the Torah was written or edited during the Babylonian captivity, 1,000 years after Moses. But the specific form of Deuteronomy was found only in treaties from around the time of Moses, making it more likely the books of the Torah really were from that period rather than later.

NEVI'IM

The second section in the Tanakh is called the Nevi'im, meaning "writings." It contains the works of the prophets that are not poetry, wisdom literature, or Chronicles. Like Moses, the prophets claimed to speak for God. And to prove their authority they did signs and wonders, often predictive prophecy. If someone claimed to be a prophet but could not prove their authority, or if they got even one prophecy wrong, then they would be stoned. Their lives were always on the line when they proclaimed the message God gave them.

In the Hebrew Bible there are eight books of the prophets: Joshua, Judges, Samuel, Kings, Isaiah, Jeremiah, Ezekiel, and the Twelve Minor Prophets. The Septuagint and the Old Testament break Samuel and Kings into two books each, and make each of the minor prophets their own book. The difference between a major and minor prophet isn't necessarily how important they were but how much they wrote. The prophets who wrote little are the minor prophets.

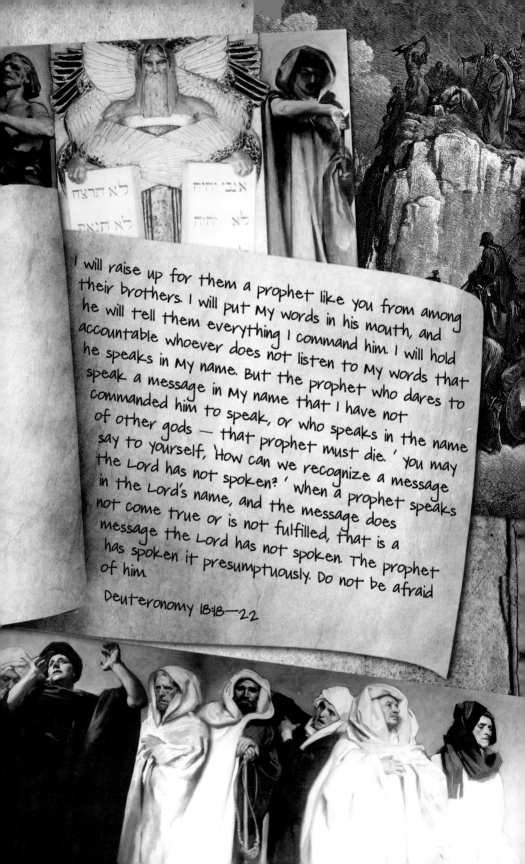

I will raise up for them a prophet like you from among their brothers. I will put My words in his mouth, and he will tell them everything I command him. I will hold accountable whoever does not listen to My words that he speaks in My name. But the prophet who dares to speak a message in My name that I have not commanded him to speak, or who speaks in the name of other gods — that prophet must die.' You may say to yourself, 'How can we recognize a message the Lord has not spoken?' when a prophet speaks in the Lord's name, and the message does not come true or is not fulfilled, that is a message the Lord has not spoken. The prophet has spoken it presumptuously. Do not be afraid of him.

Deuteronomy 18:18—22

MAJOR PROPHETS

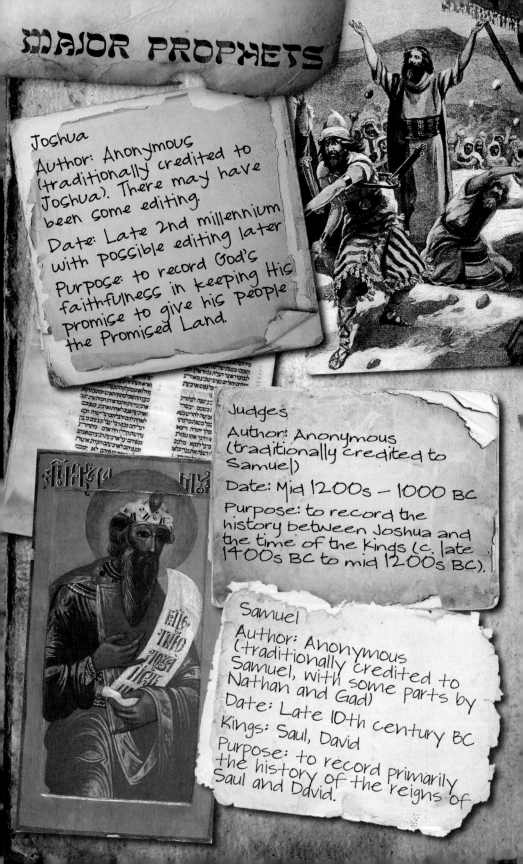

Joshua

Author: Anonymous (traditionally credited to Joshua). There may have been some editing.

Date: Late 2nd millennium with possible editing later

Purpose: to record God's faithfulness in keeping His promise to give his people the Promised Land.

Judges

Author: Anonymous (traditionally credited to Samuel)

Date: Mid 1200s – 1000 BC

Purpose: to record the history between Joshua and the time of the Kings (c. late 1400s BC to mid 1200s BC).

Samuel

Author: Anonymous (traditionally credited to Samuel, with some parts by Nathan and Gad)

Date: Late 10th century BC

Kings: Saul, David

Purpose: to record primarily the history of the reigns of Saul and David.

Kings
Author: Anonymous (traditionally credited to Jeremiah)
Date: 6th century BC with possible edits later
King: Solomon (united kingdom), Rehoboam, Abijam, Asa, Jehoshaphat (Judah), Jeroboam I, Nadab, Baasha, ...ah, Zimri, Tibni, Omri, Ahab, ...hazia(Israel)
Purpose: to record the history of Israel from 970-586 BC.

Jeremiah
Author: Jeremiah
Date: Late 7th - early 6th centuries BC
King: Josiah, Jehoahaz, Jehoiakim, Jehoiachin, Zedekiah (Judah)
Purpose: to record the history of the Late 7th - early 6th centuries BC

Isaiah
Author: Isaiah
Date: 8-7th century BC
Kings: Uzziah, Jotham, Ahaz, Hezekiah (Judah)
Purpose: to remind Israel of God's promises made to his people in order to call them back from their unbelief.

Ezekiel
Author: Ezekiel
Date: c. 593 - c. 571 BC
King: Jehoiachin, Zedekiah (Judah),
Purpose: to remind Israel of God's goodness and his promises as they suffered for turning their backs on God.

Hosea

Date: 8th century

Kingdom: Judah

King: Uzziah, Jotham, Ahaz, and Hezekiah (Judah), Jeroboam (Israel)

Purpose: To reveal how God keeps his promises even when his people have turned from him and been unfaithful

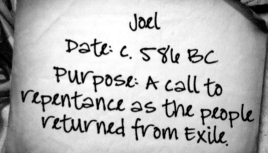

Joel

Date: c. 586 BC

Purpose: A call to repentance as the people returned from Exile.

Amos

Date: c. 750 BC

Kingdom: Israel

King: Jeroboam II, Uzziah

Purpose: To rebuke God's people of their self righteousness and warn them of God's judgment

Obadiah
Date: c. 570 BC
Purpose: To proclaim judgment on Edom and restoration for Zion

Jonah
Date: c. 760
Kingdom: Israel
King: Jeroboam II
Purpose: To emphasize God's compassion, show his desire to call Gentiles, and show how His people should reflect that compassion.

Micah
Date: c. 740
Kingdom: Judah
King: Jotham, Ahaz, Hezekiah
Purpose: To rebuke both Judah and Israel for their many sins and to proclaim judgment

MINOR PROPHETS
PT. 2

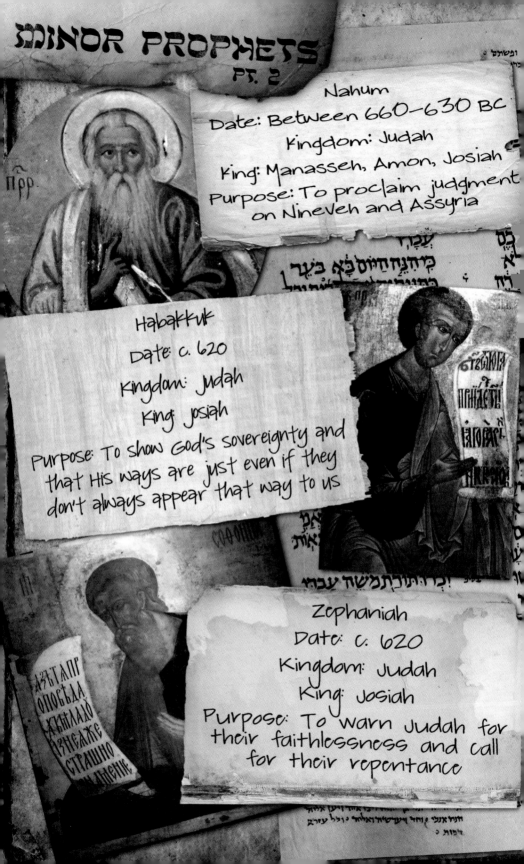

Nahum

Date: Between 660–630 BC

Kingdom: Judah

King: Manasseh, Amon, Josiah

Purpose: To proclaim judgment on Nineveh and Assyria

Habakkuk

Date: c. 620

Kingdom: Judah

King: Josiah

Purpose: To show God's sovereignty and that His ways are just even if they don't always appear that way to us

Zephaniah

Date: c. 620

Kingdom: Judah

King: Josiah

Purpose: To warn Judah for their faithlessness and call for their repentance

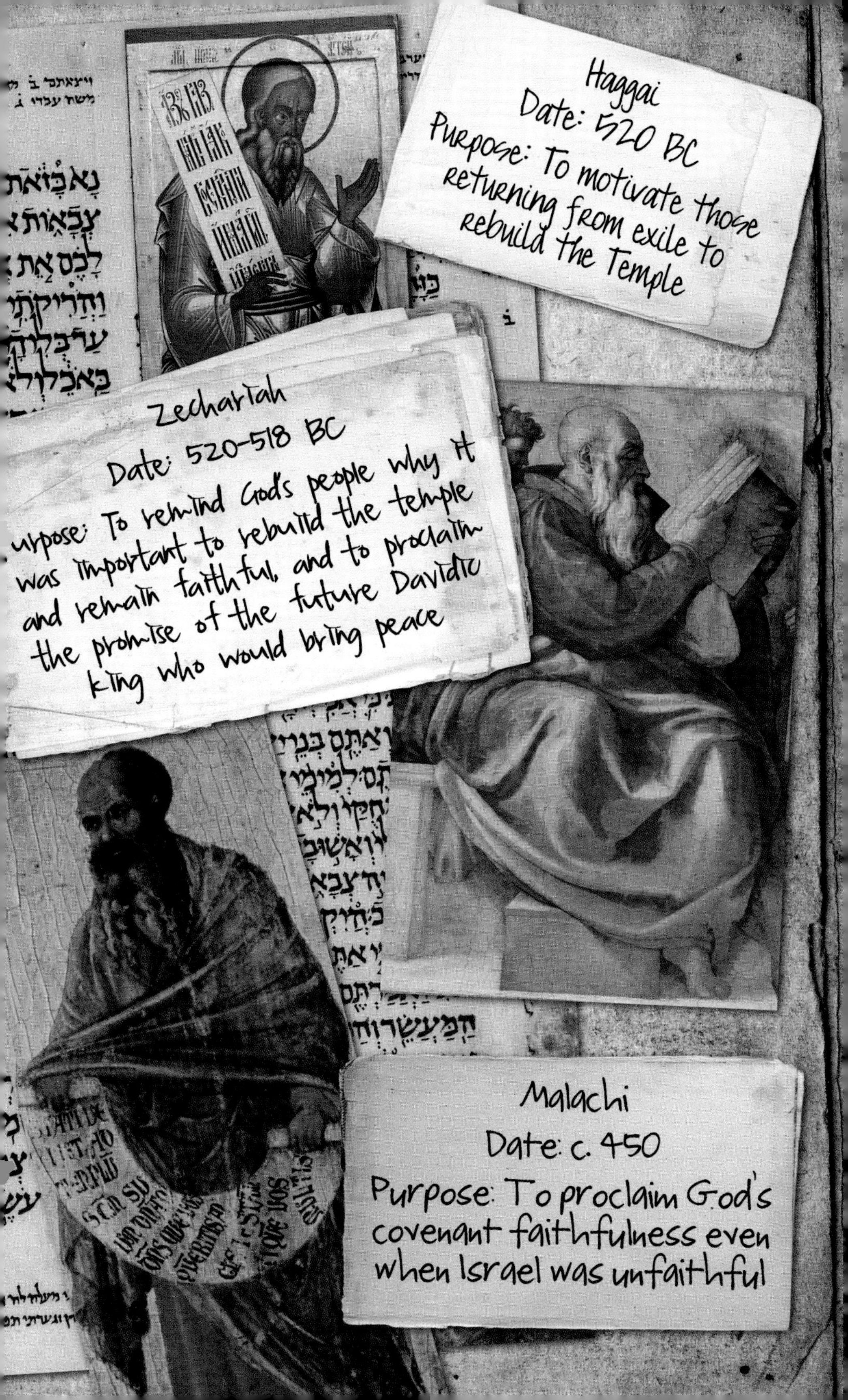

Haggai
Date: 520 BC
Purpose: To motivate those returning from exile to rebuild the Temple
Zechariah
Date: 520-518 BC
urpose: To remind God's people why it was important to rebuild the temple and remain faithful, and to proclaim the promise of the future Davidic king who would bring peace
Malachi
Date: c. 450
Purpose: To proclaim God's covenant faithfulness even when Israel was unfaithful

KETUVI'IM

The third section of the Tanahk is called the Ketuvi'im or hagiographa, which means "holy writings." Sometimes the Ketuvi'im is referred to simply as the Psalms even though it contains more than the Psalms. There are eleven books in the Ketuvi'im: Psalms, Proverbs, Job, the Five Scrolls (Song of Songs, Ruth, Lamentations, Ecclesiastes, and Esther), Daniel, Ezra/Nehemiah, and Chronicles.

Even though all of scripture is inspired by God and is authoritative, Jews don't think of the Ketuvi'im as being as important as the Nevi'im, and neither of them are as important as the Torah. Some Jewish sects, such as the Samaritans and the Sadducees, rejected both the Ketuvi'im and the Nevi'im as inspired writing.

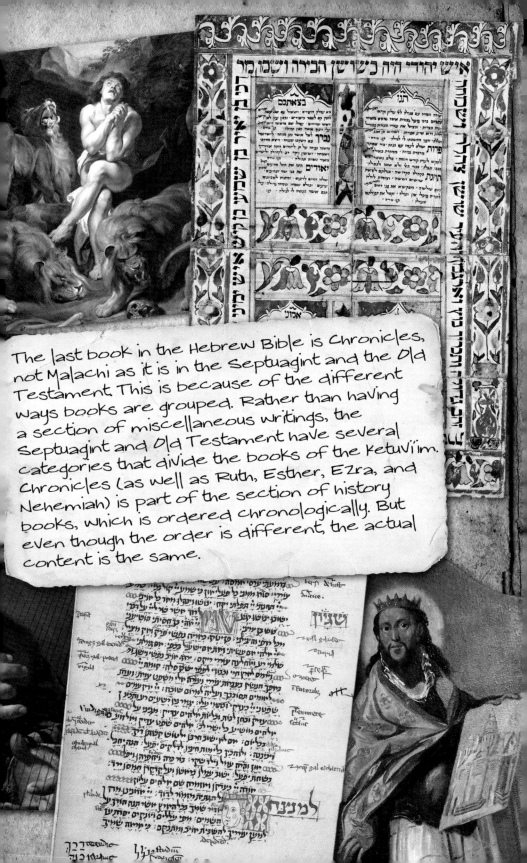

The last book in the Hebrew Bible is Chronicles, not Malachi as it is in the Septuagint and the Old Testament This is because of the different ways books are grouped. Rather than having a section of miscellaneous writings, the Septuagint and Old Testament have several categories that divide the books of the Ketuvi'im. Chronicles (as well as Ruth, Esther, Ezra, and Nehemiah) is part of the section of history books, which is ordered chronologically. But even though the order is different, the actual content is the same.

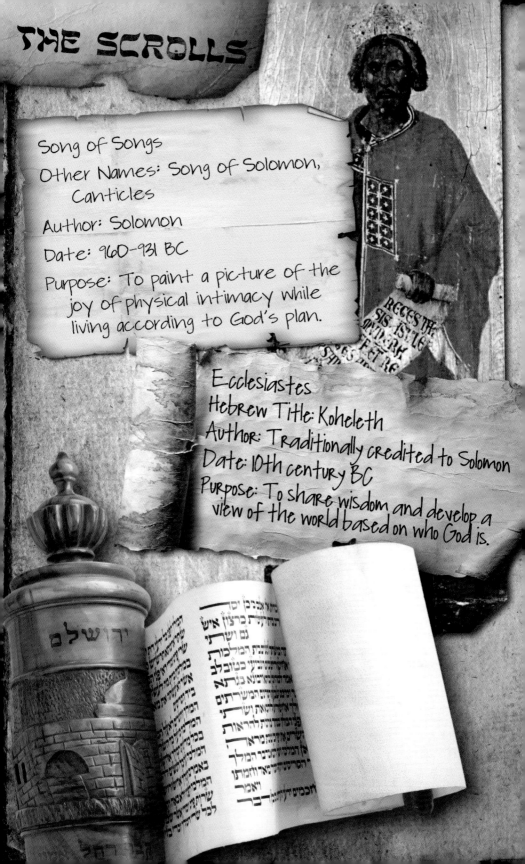

THE SCROLLS

Song of Songs

Other Names: Song of Solomon, Canticles

Author: Solomon

Date: 960-931 BC

Purpose: To paint a picture of the joy of physical intimacy while living according to God's plan.

Ecclesiastes

Hebrew Title: Koheleth

Author: Traditionally credited to Solomon

Date: 10th century BC

Purpose: To share wisdom and develop a view of the world based on who God is.

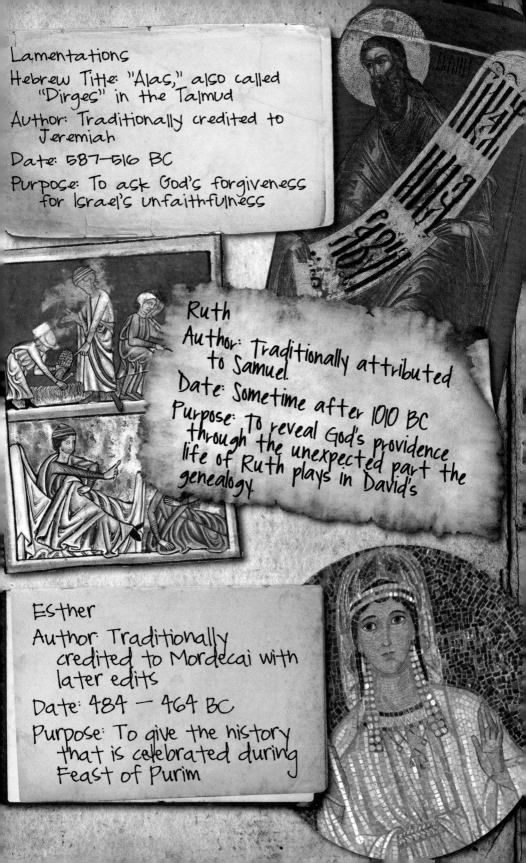

Lamentations

Hebrew Title: "Alas," also called "Dirges" in the Talmud

Author: Traditionally credited to Jeremiah

Date: 587–516 BC

Purpose: To ask God's forgiveness for Israel's unfaithfulness

Ruth

Author: Traditionally attributed to Samuel.

Date: Sometime after 1010 BC

Purpose: To reveal God's providence through the unexpected part the life of Ruth plays in David's genealogy.

Esther

Author: Traditionally credited to Mordecai with later edits

Date: 484 – 464 BC

Purpose: To give the history that is celebrated during Feast of Purim

WISDOM BOOKS

Psalms
Hebrew Title: Tehillim (Hymns of Praise)
Authors: David and other worship leaders
Date: 15th cent BC – 5th cent BC
Purpose: A collection of hymns used by Israel in worship

Proverbs
Hebrew Title: Mishlei
Author: Solomon
Date: 10th cent BC
Purpose: To convey the wisdom of placing God as the center of all of life, how His plan for how we should live acts against the effects of the fall.

Job
Author: Traditionally credited to Moses
Date: 15th cent BC – 6th century BC depending on the author
Purpose: To show how an all-powerful, sovereign, good, and just God can exist even though we are tempted to question him when we experience suffering

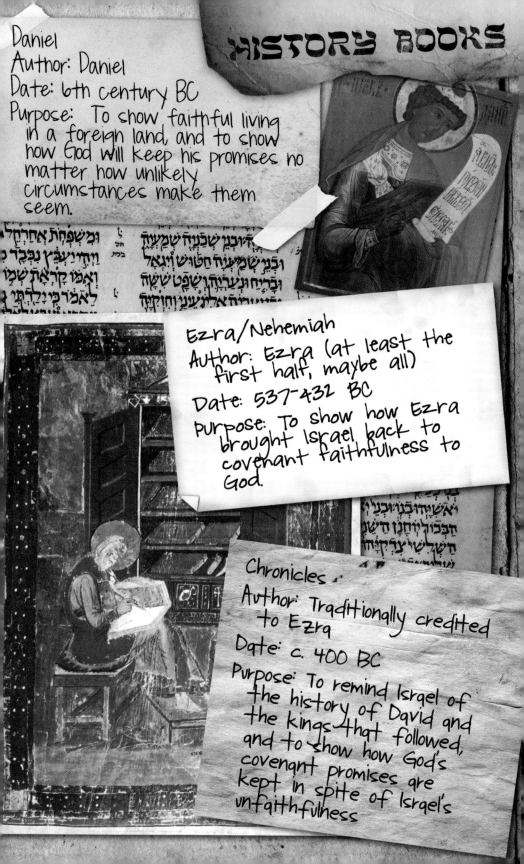

Daniel
Author: Daniel
Date: 6th century BC
Purpose: To show faithful living in a foreign land, and to show how God will keep his promises no matter how unlikely circumstances make them seem.

Ezra/Nehemiah
Author: Ezra (at least the first half, maybe all)
Date: 537-432 BC
Purpose: To show how Ezra brought Israel back to covenant faithfulness to God.

Chronicles
Author: Traditionally credited to Ezra
Date: c. 400 BC
Purpose: To remind Israel of the history of David and the kings that followed, and to show how God's covenant promises are kept in spite of Israel's unfaithfulness

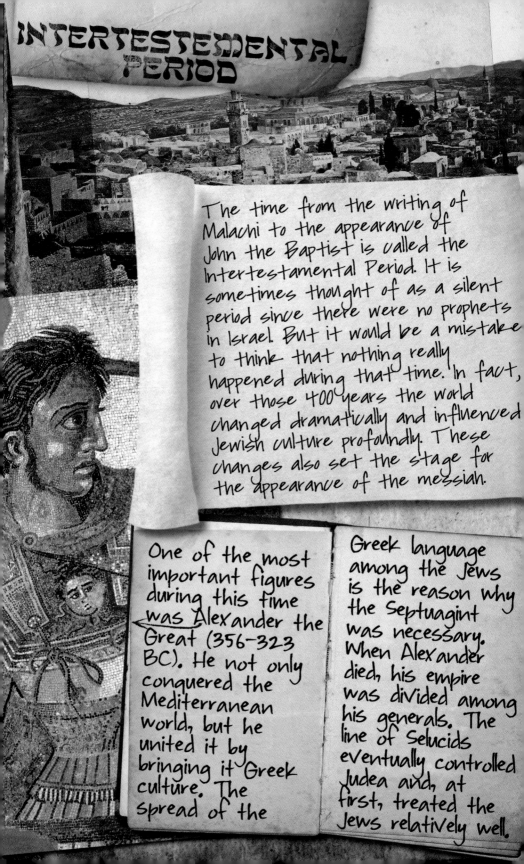

The time from the writing of Malachi to the appearance of John the Baptist is called the Intertestamental Period. It is sometimes thought of as a silent period since there were no prophets in Israel. But it would be a mistake to think that nothing really happened during that time. In fact, over those 400 years the world changed dramatically and influenced Jewish culture profoundly. These changes also set the stage for the appearance of the messiah.

One of the most important figures during this time was Alexander the Great (356-323 BC). He not only conquered the Mediterranean world, but he united it by bringing it Greek culture. The spread of the Greek language among the Jews is the reason why the Septuagint was necessary. When Alexander died, his empire was divided among his generals. The line of Selucids eventually controlled Judea and, at first, treated the Jews relatively well.

When Antiochus IV ruled from 175 - 164 BC, he tried to get rid of anything in his empire (which included Judea) that wasn't part of Greek culture. He made Judaism illegal, converted the temple to worship of pagan gods, and destroyed the walls of Jerusalem. This led to a revolt by ↓ the Jews that reclaimed Judea and the temple, an event celebrated during Hannakuh, the Feast of Dedication. This persecution and others that followed created a desire for a military leader to rise up and free Israel. Many Jews even began to expect the messiah prophesied in scripture to lead a rebellion.

After the Romans conquered Judea in 63 BC, they allowed the Jews to govern themselves for the most part. In 47 BC, Herod was named governor of Galilee, and within ten years expanded his rule to include the whole region. He became known as Herod the Great because of his many building programs which included the rebuilding of the temple in Jerusalem. It was during his reign that Jesus was born. And it was during his son Herod's time as governor of Galilee that Jesus was crucified.

APOCRYPHA

There were many important books written during the Intertestamental period. Jewish history is well documented during that time. There were also books containing wisdom and prophecy. But even though these books were important to the Jews, they did not consider them as authoritative as Scripture and were never part of the canon. They are called the Apocrypha, meaning "hidden" because they were not included in the canon.

Judith
Tobit
Susannah

There are 14 books in the Apocrypha: 1 Maccabees, 2 Maccabees, 1 Esdras, 2 Esdras, Ecclesiasticus, Wisdom of Solomon, Tobit, Judith, Prayer of Manasseh, additional verses to Esther, Bel and the Dragon, Song of the Three Holy Children, The History of Susannah, and Baruch (chapter 6 is 6 is called the Epistle of Jeremiah). Sometimes 3 and 4 Maccabees are also included in the Apocrypha. The books were important enough to the Jews that they are included at the end of the Septuagint even though they were not considered scripture.

The Roman Catholic Church includes most of these books in their Bible. Tobit and Judith follow Nehemiah, Wisdom of Solomon and Ecclesiasticus follow the Song of Songs, and Baruch follows Lamentations. Esther contains additional verses, and the other three books are added to the end of Daniel. This makes the Roman Catholic Old Testament 46 books rather than the 39 the early church favored and that Protestants use.

Baruch

The Greek Orthodox Church still uses the Septuagint as the translation of the Hebrew Bible and therefore includes the all of the Apocrypha in their Bibles, though (like Roman Catholics) they refer to the books as Deuterocanonical, meaning "second canon." Four books rejected by Roman Catholics are included: 1 Esdras (also called 3 Esdras), 2 Esdras (also called 4 Esdras), Prayer of Manasseh, Psalm 151.

VULGATE

As Christianity spread so did the need for copies of the scriptures in various languages. The most important translation was in Latin since it was so widely used. But often the Latin versions, which started in the late 2nd century, were not very good. In 382, Damasus, the bishop of Rome, realized the need for a standard or common Latin translation. To take on this translation, he enlisted one of the great biblical scholars of the early church, a bishop from Antioch named Jerome.

Jerome (c. 347-420) had received an excellent education in Rome and had mastered both Greek and Latin before devoting himself to ministry. He also spent several years as a hermit outside of Antioch, during which he learned Hebrew and Aramaic. By 384 he had translated the four Gospels and the Psalms, though he had translated the Psalms from the Septuagint and not the original Hebrew. After Damasus died in 384, Jerome settled in Bethlehem in the same caves where Jesus is traditionally thought to have been born.

Jerome continued his translation of the old Testament into Latin but decided to use the original Hebrew for the text, while keeping the organization of the Septuagint. In order to make sure his translation was as accurate as possible, Jerome consulted with several Jewish teachers as he worked. It was through their instruction he came to understand that the Septuagint included books that were important to the Jews but were not considered scripture.

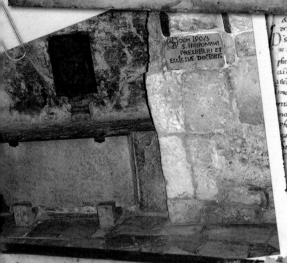

In his introduction to Samuel and Kings he lists the canon of the Hebrew Bible so it would be clear to anyone reading his translation just what was included in scripture. He also names books that belong to the Apocrypha rather than scripture. He does, however, say they are edifying books for the church even though doctrine should not be taken from them. He also notes that his view follows the Jews, and that they reject these books from the canon. In the end, he translated Tobit and Judith from Aramaic, and included the rest of the Apocrypha in their existing Latin form without doing a new translation. The result of Jerome's work is called the Latin Vulgate, meaning the common Latin version.

APOCRYPHA ACCEPTANCE

How to treat the books that were included at the end of the Septuagint but not in the Hebrew Bible was something that Christians dealt with long before Jerome's Latin Vulgate. The oldest list of the Old Testament books comes from a homily written by Melito of Sardis in AD 170. He includes every book but Esther, and excludes all of the Apocrypha. however, important early copies of the Old Testament — such as Siniaticus, Vaticanus, and Alexandrinus — all include at least some of the books of the Apocrypha.

The early church fathers had differing opinions. Tertullian (160-220) seems to accept a number of the apocryphal books. Origen (185-254) lists all 22 Hebrew books, though he seems to include the Letter of Jeremiah at the end of Jeremiah. Athanasius (296-373), who created the oldest complete list of the New Testament books, also listed the Old Testament books in the same letter. He also included the Letter of Jeremiah and Baruch, but excluded Esther. And Augustine (354-430) seemed to accept the Septuagint's list. The Council of Carthage (398), the first council to publish a list of canonical books, included the apocrypha.

Before Jerome's Latin Vulgate became widely accepted, many Christians were suspicious of it because it was different from the Latin translation of the Septuagint they were used to. The idea of not accepting some of the books included in the Septuagint was difficult for them to get used to. Even by the Middle Ages the church was trying to decide just how to treat the books of the Apocrypha, with some people or Bibles accepting them and others not.

In the mid 12th century, Hugh of St Victor Abbey taught that the Apocrypha was not part of the canon. He also taught that there was a tradition of scholars from the early church who all rejected the Apocrypha. John Wycliffe did include the Apocrypha in his 14th century translation because it followed Jerome's Vulgate. But like Jerome, Wycliffe distinguishes between the canon and the additional books.

APOCRYPHA CANONIZATION

The exact definition of what books Christians in the Western world believed should belong to the Old Testament wasn't finally decided until the Reformation. One of Martin Luther's main complaints against the Roman Church was that it considered tradition to be as authoritative as scripture itself. But Luther believed many of Rome's traditions were in conflict with scripture

and criticized Rome based on the principle of Sola Scriptura, that scripture alone should be the only rule of faith and practice. By taking that stand he believed he had scriptural grounds for rejecting the church's teaching on purgatory (a place of temporary punishment for sins before being allowed into paradise), indulgences (a fee that reduced time in purgatory), and prayers for the dead.

Roman theologians pointed out that all these doctrines were indeed found in scripture and cited books from the Apocrypha. Luther, citing Jerome as his authority, showed that the Apocryphal books were not to be considered scripture and therefore should not be used to make doctrine. Interestingly, when he translated the Bible into German he included the Apocrypha in its own section with a note saying the books were important but not to be read as scripture. Other Protestant Bibles followed Luther's example but often began placing them between the Old and New Testaments.

In response to many of the concerns of the Reformation, the Roman Catholic Church held a council at Trent in 1545. The council decided the most authoritative version of the Latin form of the Bible was the one that existed before Jerome. And because the earliest form of the Latin Bible treated all the books equally instead of dividing them, like Jerome into Scripture and merely important books, the Council decided it shouldn't divide them either. As a result, the Apocrypha – books rejected by the Jews from their own canon – was canonized by the Roman Catholic Church.

About 100 years later, the eastern orthodox church also made an official pronouncement on the canon at the councils of Jassy (1642) and Jerusalem (1672). They believed the Septuagint itself was an inspired translation and that in the parts where it disagrees with the Hebrew Bible's text, the Septuagint is the correct reading. They also accepted all the books of the Apocrypha, including several rejected by the Roman Catholic church. However, many orthodox theologians no longer believe the apocryphal books should be treated as highly as the rest of scripture.

DEAD SEA SCROLLS

The greatest archaeological discovery of the 20th century happened in late 1946 or early 1947 when a shepherd looking for a lost goat found a cave that held several ancient scrolls and thousands of fragments from other scrolls. Over the next 10 years 10 other caves containing scrolls were discovered in the same area along the coast of the Dead sea, southeast of Jerusalem.

Cave 1

Over 100,000 scrolls or fragments of scrolls were found that belonged to over 900 different books and writings. At least 223 of the books were copies of the Hebrew Bible. The reason this is so important is that before this discovery, the oldest copies of the Tanakh were from the 10th century AD. But the copies of the Tanakh from the Dead sea scrolls date from 150 BC to AD 70. At least one copy of every book in the Tanakh was discovered except for Esther.

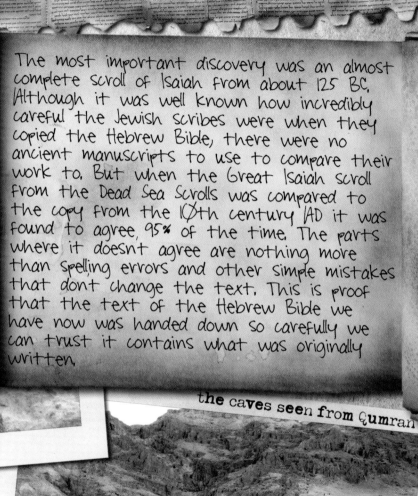

The most important discovery was an almost complete scroll of Isaiah from about 125 BC. Although it was well known how incredibly careful the Jewish scribes were when they copied the Hebrew Bible, there were no ancient manuscripts to use to compare their work to. But when the Great Isaiah scroll from the Dead Sea Scrolls was compared to the copy from the 10th century AD it was found to agree, 95% of the time. The parts where it doesn't agree are nothing more than spelling errors and other simple mistakes that don't change the text. This is proof that the text of the Hebrew Bible we have now was handed down so carefully we can trust it contains what was originally written.

the caves seen from Qumran

ARCHAEOLOGY

The Bible claims to record real events in history. However, the Bible has often been the only record we have of certain events, people, or nations. Some skeptics have used the lack of non-biblical evidence to say the Bible's history is not trustworthy. But since the rise of archaeology in the 18th century there have been many discoveries that have backed up the history in the Bible. Here are a few of the most important finds.

The Tel Dan Stele (9th cent BC) is part of a victory monument discovered in Israel that mentions the House of David. This is evidence that King David actually existed and was an important figure in the region.

The Cyrus Cylinder (6th cent BC) was found in Babylon in 1879. It is a record of Cyrus's military victories and mentions how he let captives return to their homeland. That agrees with 2 Chron 36:22-23; Isaiah 45:1-13, and Ezra 1:1-3, 6:1-5.

The Merneptah Stele (13th cent BC) is a monument found in Thebes, Egypt, that mentions the name "Israel." It's the oldest record of the name outside the Bible.

The Black Obelisk of Shalmaneser III (9th cent BC) has a picture of King Jehu paying tribute to Shalmaneser III. This is the oldest picture of an Israelite and was made during Jehu's lifetime.

NEW TESTAMENT

What does the Hebrew Bible have to do with the New Testament? For Jews the answer is nothing. At best, Jesus was a well-meaning teacher who was profoundly mistaken about his own authority. The New Testament is useful only as a picture of the heretical sect that grew from his teachings and what the Jewish world was like at that time.

But Christians believe the New Testament is the final revelation of God's Word and is inseparable from the Hebrew Bible. And the main reason they treat the Hebrew Bible as scripture is because Jesus did. In his arguments with Pharisees, Sadducees, and scribes, Jesus frequently quoted the Tanakh as scripture. Sometimes he refers to it as the Law, the Prophets, and the Psalms (what the Writings were sometimes called) which shows he held the same books as scripture they did. The religious leaders never argued about which books were scripture; they only argued about their interpretation. The reason Christians believe Jesus was telling the truth about the Hebrew Bible is because of his resurrection from the dead which proved he was telling the truth about himself and whatever else he taught.

On the day Jesus was resurrected, one of the first appearances he made was to two of his followers traveling to Emmaus. Jesus explained to them how he was found all throughout the Tanakh. He showed how he fulfilled all the requirements of the law, how he was who the temple sacrificial ceremonies pointed to, how he was the promised Messiah, and how he was the central figure of the Hebrew Bible. People before Christ were saved through faith in his promised coming, people after Christ are saved by faith in the promise kept. It's the Hebrew Bible that puts Jesus in the right context so he can be recognized as the Messiah.

The New Testament quotes the Hebrew Bible at least 295 times and alludes to it many more times. And every quote is an appeal to it as authoritative scripture. The New Testament writers did not see themselves as creating something new that had nothing to do with Judaism. They saw themselves as recording how God fulfilled all his promises through Jesus and how the good news of God's faithfulness began to spread throughout the world. And that good news will continue to be spread until the return of Jesus Christ.

TIMELINE

— TIME OF JUDGES —

Othniel (1377–1337)

Ehud (1319–1239)

Shamgar (?)

Deborah (1239–1199)

Gideon (1192–1152)

Tola (1149–1126)

Jair (1126–1104)

Jephthah (1086–1080)

Ibzan (1080–1072)

Elon (1072–1062)

Abdon (1062–1055)

Samson (1075–1055)

— EARLY HISTORY —

Creation

Adam

Noah

Abraham (2166–1991)

Isaac (2066–1886)

Jacob (2006–1859)

Joseph (1915–1805)

Moses (1526–1406)

Exodus (c. 1446)

Joshua (ruled 1406–1385)

TIME OF KINGS
Saul (c.1025-1010)
David (1010-971)
Solomon (971-931)

SOUTHERN KINGDOM (JUDAH)
Rehoboam (931-913)
Abijam (931-911)
Asa (911-870)
Jehoshaphat (873-848)
Jehoram (853-841)
Ahaziah (841)
Athaliah (841-835)
Joash (835-796)
Amaziah (796-767)
Azariah (792-740)
Jotham (750-732)
Ahaz (735-716)
Hezekiah (716-687)
Manasseh (697-643)
Amon (643-641)
Josiah (641-609)
Jehoahaz (609)
Jehoiakim (609-598)
Jehoiachin (598-597)

NORTHERN KINGDOM (ISRAEL)
Jeroboam I (931-910)
Nadab (910-909)
Baasha (909-886)
Elah (886-885)
Zimri (885)
Tibni (?)
Omri (885-874)
Ahab (874-853)
Ahaziah (853-852)
Joram (852-841)
Jehu (841-814)
Jehoahaz (814-789)
Jehoash (798-782)
Jeroboam II (793-753)
Zachariah (753-752)
Shallum (752)
Menahem (752-742)
Pekahiah (742-740)
Pekah (752-732)
Hoshea (723-722)

Assyrian Captivity - Northern Kingdom (734)
Babylonian Captivity - Southern Kingdom (608-586)
Return from exile (538-428)
Temple Completed (515)
Seleucid I (312-281)
Maccabbean Revolt (160)
Herod (40 - 4 BC)
Jesus (4-6 BC - AD 30/33)

BIBLIOGRAPHY

Apologetics Study Bible (Nashville: Holman Bible Publishers, 2007)

Bowman, Robert, *Scripture: Authority, Canon, and Criticism*, Syllabus for CSAP529 (La Mirada, CA: Biola University Bookstore)

Bruce, F.F., *The Canon of Scripture* (Downers Grove, ILL: IVP Academic, 1988)

Encyclopedia of the Jewish Religion, R.J. Zwi Weblowsky and Geoffery Wigoder, eds. (New York: Hold, Rinehart, Winston, 1965)

ESV Study Bible (Wheaton, Ill: Crossway, 2008)

Grudem, Wayne, *Systematic Theology* (Grand Rapids: Zondervan, 1994, 2000)

Habel, Norman, *Literary Criticism of the Old Testament* (Philadelphia: Fortress, 1971)

Holman Illustrated Bible Dictionary (Nashville: Holman Bible Publishers, 2003)

Jewish Study Bible (Oxford: Oxford University Press, 1985, 1999)

Longman, Tremper, III, and Raymond B. Dillard, *An Introduction to the Old Testament* (Grand Rapids: Zondervan, 1994, 2006)

McDowell, Josh, *Evidence that Demands a Verdict vol II* (San Bernadino, CA: Here's Life, 1975, 1989)

New Jerusalem Bible (New York: Doubleday, 1990)

New Oxford Annotated Bible with Apocrypha (New York: Oxford University Press, 1962, 1977)

Price, Matthew A., and Michael Collins, *The Story of Christianity* (Wheaton: Tyndale, 1999)

Walton, John H., *Charts of The Old Testament* (Grand Rapids: Zondervan, 1978, 1994)

Who's Who in the Bible, Joan Comay and Ronald Brownrigg, eds. (New York: Wings, 1971)

Wilkinson, Bruce, and Robert Boa, *The Wilkinson & Boa Bible Handbook* (Nashville: Thomas Nelson, 1983, 2002)

http://www.jewishencyclopedia.com/articles/3259-bible-canon (accessed 11/15/2013)

Cover: Book background: © iStockphoto

Background on all pages: Public Domain

Title page: Illustrations: Public Domain; Scroll:
   © Dreamstime

Intro
   Blank scroll: © Dreamstime; Illuminated manuscript, Nash
   Papyrus and Paintings: Public Domain; Paper clipped paper
   and Scroll: © iStockphoto

Manuscripts
   Paper: © Dreamstime; Tags: © iStockphoto; Talmud, Torah
   scroll: Public Domain;

Copying
   Photo frame, bottom right paper, Taped paper:
   © iStockphoto; Paper: © Dreamstime; Scribes: Public
   Domain; Writing materials: Pete Unseth (CC BY SA 3);

Canon Criteria
   Icon, Painting, and Title page: Public Domain; Paper
   backgrounds: © Dreamstime; Paper scraps: © iStockphoto

Canon Formation
   Artwork and Talmud: Public Domain; Book spread and
   Scroll: © Dreamstime; Paper (bottom two scraps): ©
   ba1969/sxc.hu; Paper (middle right): © loompus/sxc.hu;
   White paper scrap: © iStockphoto;

Septuagint
   Artwork and Papyrus: Public Domain; Paper: © iStockphoto;
   Paper (bottom left): © Dreamstime

Torah
   Artwork: Public Domain; Books: © Dreamstime; Paper:
   © iStockphoto; Torah Scroll: Lawrie Cate (CC 2.0)

Prophets
   Artwork: Public Domain; Paper: © Dreamstime

Documentary Hypothesis
   Artwork and photos: Public Domain; Paper: © Dreamstime;
   Photo frame: © iStockphoto.

Covenants
   Amarna Letter: CaptMondo (CC-BY 2.5); Public Domain;
   Mari Tablet: Jastro (Public Domain) ; Paper: © Dreamstime

Nevi'im
   Artwork and manuscript: Public Domain; Paper:
   © Dreamstime

Major Prophets
   Artwork and manuscript: Public Domain; Paper:
   © Dreamstime

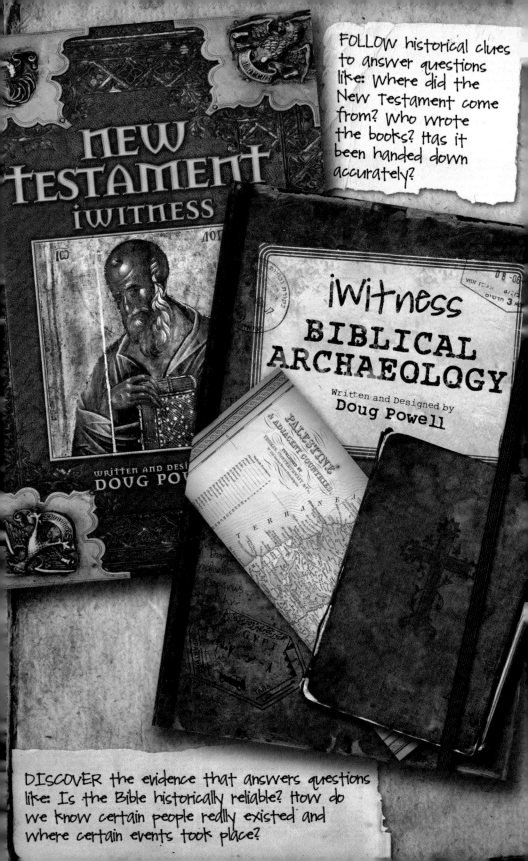

FOLLOW historical clues to answer questions like: Where did the New Testament come from? Who wrote the books? Has it been handed down accurately?

NEW TESTAMENT iWITNESS

WRITTEN AND DESIGNED BY
DOUG POWELL

iWitness BIBLICAL ARCHAEOLOGY

Written and Designed by
Doug Powell

DISCOVER the evidence that answers questions like: Is the Bible historically reliable? How do we know certain people really existed and where certain events took place?

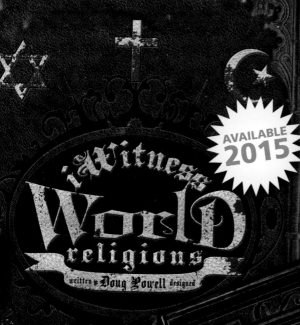

iWitness WORLD religions

written by Doug Powell designed

AVAILABLE 2015

EXPLORE the most popular religions in the world to answer the question, "What do different religions teach about God, the world, people, what's wrong with the world, and what is the solution?"

iWitness Heresies & Cults

WRITTEN DOUG POWELL DESIGN

AVAILABLE 2015

INVESTIGATE early church history to find out what is meant by orthodoxy, heresy, and cult. Then see how different cults of Christianity always teach heresies condemned over 1,500 years ago.

iWitness Books by Doug Powell from

✝ apologia.